Affirmations

500+ Daily Affirmations for Positive Thinking, Success, Money, Love, Happiness, Focus, Abundance, Self-Esteem, and Motivation

© **Copyright 2019**

All Rights Reserved. No part of this book may be reproduced in any form without permission in writing from the author. Reviewers may quote brief passages in reviews.

Disclaimer: No part of this publication may be reproduced or transmitted in any form or by any means, mechanical or electronic, including photocopying or recording, or by any information storage and retrieval system, or transmitted by email without permission in writing from the publisher.

While all attempts have been made to verify the information provided in this publication, neither the author nor the publisher assumes any responsibility for errors, omissions or contrary interpretations of the subject matter herein.

This book is for entertainment purposes only. The views expressed are those of the author alone, and should not be taken as expert instruction or commands. The reader is responsible for his or her own actions.

Adherence to all applicable laws and regulations, including international, federal, state and local laws governing professional licensing, business practices, advertising and all other aspects of doing business in the US, Canada, UK or any other jurisdiction is the sole responsibility of the purchaser or reader.

Neither the author nor the publisher assumes any responsibility or liability whatsoever on the behalf of the purchaser or reader of these materials. Any perceived slight of any individual or organization is purely unintentional.

1. I can easily let go of my past and stay focused on the present.
2. I choose to be happy.
3. I am so happy and grateful that money easily flows to me from all directions continuously.
4. I maximize every hour in the day by being productive.
5. My home is a clean, warm, and happy place that supports my wellbeing.
6. I am beautiful, kind, unique, powerful, and capable.
7. I love and believe in me right here and right now, and by definition, I have tremendous wealth, absolute happiness, abundance, and expansive ideas that elevate my life.
8. My life has purpose and meaning.
9. I am worth it, valuable, and important.
10. I have no fear of taking risks and working in different directions, and I celebrate that about myself.
11. I can accomplish anything; I simply need to begin. Nothing stops me from starting a task, and once I start, I can accomplish all that I need to.
12. My procrastination melts away by using my time wisely and staying organized.
13. I am always peaceful and relaxed.
14. My riches, both in money and experience, are plentiful.
15. I free myself from anyone or anything that is toxic to my wellbeing.
16. My positive money visions are coming true.
17. Money is attracted to me. I am a winner, and I am successful.
18. Today is a new beginning that is filled with many opportunities.
19. I am confident, creative, beautiful, blessed, and excited about my future.
20. I focus on relationships that are positive, healthy, and make me feel loved and respected.
21. People love me and love to be around me.

22. I express my full potential daily and am geared for success.
23. I am a fearless, deserving, self-supporting leader who is creating peace and stability in my life.
24. I am an alluring magnet with the incredible ability to attain everything I want in life.
25. I have an ocean of love, courage, and strength inside, and it grows with every sunrise.
26. I see the good in every situation.
27. I am very capable of managing any challenges that come my way.
28. My plan of action is not swayed by uncertainty.
29. There is no such thing as disappointment in my life as I only set realistic expectations.
30. I am at peace, and allowing my body to recharge.
31. My body and mind will be ready to take on new challenges once I have given it the rest it needs and deserves.
32. I am attracting the right people and circumstances to achieve my perfect career.
33. I improve myself every day, every hour, and every minute.
34. I am responsible for my actions.
35. I embrace the abundance of the universe, and now, all my needs are taken care of.
36. My life has a positive impact on the world.
37. My determination will let me achieve anything I put my mind to.
38. I choose to be happy, free-spirited, full of energy, and at peace.
39. I am filled with energy to do all of my daily tasks.
40. Plenty of money is flowing into my life.
41. I free myself from negativity and toxic relationships.
42. I fully approve of who I am, even as I get better.
43. I am prepared to live the rest of my life for myself and not for anyone else.
44. I am confident in my abilities to accumulate wealth and manage it intelligently.

45. I am comfortable with my life the way that it is and excess plays no role in my life.
46. I am happy within myself, and my possessions are merely bonuses to my already overflowing happiness.
47. The universe adores me; everything always works out exactly in my favor.
48. I am in control of my choices, and everything I do is my choice.
49. I am kind to everyone, even when it is difficult.
50. I am smart and strong enough; I can do this.
51. I am excited about my daily exercise routine.
52. My eyes are open to all the opportunities set in my path to allow me to reach my goals.
53. I offer time, love, and support to my family and friends; in turn, I receive these from everyone around me.
54. I am a great leader; I am helping others to be better today.
55. I am accepting wealth into my life.
56. I take responsibility for my happiness and take complete control over my mood.
57. I continue to improve every day and know that I have improved since this time last year.
58. I honor my desires and will always ask for what I want.
59. I am blessed with the ability to deal with any obstacles that may come my way, no matter the difficulty.
60. I have the strength to walk my own path even if others are unsupportive
61. I am experiencing every moment of my life with awareness and gratitude.
62. I am more than enough; I am perfect exactly as I am.
63. I have the right to have my needs and wants respected by others.
64. I am the happiest, healthiest me I can be.
65. I am allowing love in my life, and I deserve to have love in my life.

66. This is a great day; it is my opportunity to "show up" as my best self for the world to see.
67. My life is full of love, appreciation, respect, and happiness; I share this with myself and others.
68. I do small and simple things every day that ensure my inner peace and personal power.
69. I am trusting, know when to "let go", and have faith and belief in myself.
70. My words, thoughts, and actions are always positive.
71. Joy, ease, happiness, laughter, and love define me.
72. My views create my reality; I am choosing abundant health, infinite wealth, eternal happiness, and everlasting love.
73. I am moving towards my goals every day.
74. My thoughts are filled with positivity, and my life is filled to the brim with contentment.
75. Staying positive is easy for me.
76. I am committed to personal improvement and am always finding new ways to better myself.
77. I am thankful for the chance to serve my fellow humankind and gladly accept the riches being sent to me by a plentiful universe.
78. I am aware of my beauty, and I see the beauty in others.
79. I am satisfied with my life; I have everything I need to live a fulfilling life.
80. I approach each task with a determination to find and follow the most productive and efficient means of completing it.
81. I love taking action, and I feel courageous and exhilarated by taking action.
82. I am aligned to and ready to receive that which I want and is for my highest good.
83. I am highly focused on achieving wealth.
84. I attract financial abundance.
85. I radiate beauty, charm, and grace.
86. I am following my passions and dreams each day.

87. I am thankful for my life and body and how each part of me comes together to make me the wonderful being I am.
88. I always have the perfect home and I am perfectly at home wherever I am.
89. I have an amazingly supportive, kind, and loving family that gives me a strong foundation.
90. I increase my output by concentrating my energy and focusing my attention on the job at hand.
91. I commit to enjoying the full capacity of my love and creativity.
92. I have the time, energy, wisdom, and wealth to accomplish my goals.
93. I am healthy in mind, body, and spirit. The decisions I make are powerful and support my healthiest self.
94. I am responsible for me and how I respond.
95. I have a clear and glorious vision for my life that I will achieve.
96. I am a source of positive change in the world and bring value to all that I do.
97. Life is what I choose to see and make of what and whom I encounter along the way, so I choose wisely and mindfully.
98. People are amazed by the quality and creativity of my work.
99. As I let my light shine, I unconsciously give other people the ability to do the same.
100. I am ready for a positive, strong, and loving relationship.
101. I am embracing who I am and sharing my infectious positive attitude with others around me.
102. I am self-motivated and constantly moving forward all the time.
103. I learn from the past and focus on improving myself for the future.
104. I start every day with preparing and planning and trust myself to work diligently and effectively.

105. I let go of all distractions and improve my focus to complete my tasks.
106. I relive my stress by creating inner peace and knowledge that this too shall pass.
107. I am a hard worker, and the path to greater success is very easy for me.
108. I communicate with people easily; I use this to excel in and achieve my goals.
109. I am grateful for my ability to create new relationships.
110. My body heals itself every day, and I take good care of my mind and my body so I can grow emotionally and physically.
111. I build my self-confidence to excel and succeed. My confidence in myself is consistently growing.
112. I am very organized and focused, which helps me to be productive.
113. Every day, I focus on developing and expanding my abilities. I am getting better and better in everything I do.
114. I love what I do, and my work doesn't feel like work.
115. I have all the abilities I need to win inside of me.
116. It is easy for me to listen to people and make them feel understood.
117. I find so many meaningful moments in my job that give me a sense of purpose and fulfillment.
118. I grow my confidence by accepting myself and loving myself unconditionally.
119. I keep myself physically fit, and I wake up every morning a day younger than yesterday.
120. I prioritize my happiness and compromising my happiness is not an option.
121. I am beautiful on the inside and outside.
122. I can overcome any illness.
123. I take good care of my body through eating right and exercise.
124. My mind is at peace, and every night, I can stay asleep.

125. My only enemy is myself, and I refuse to stop myself from achieving my goals.
126. My mind is focused on the top priorities, and my ability to organize accelerates my growth.
127. I see failure as a friend that teaches me so that I can create the best version of myself.
128. I focus one step at a time; it gives me the quality of life I want.
129. I am born to win, and I use my gifts every day to create success for myself and others.
130. I am a unique person, I have special qualities, and I am on my way to success.
131. I love people, and they love me back. I understand that relating to other people is crucial for success.
132. I am grateful for this day and am excited for all the opportunities it has to offer.
133. I live today like I live every day, with peace, tranquility, joy, and pleasure.
134. I do not need anyone else to complete me as I am fully complete just the way I am.
135. I push all my fears aside and take action instead because I know this is the best way to move forward.
136. I am a positive influence on others, and am committed to living a life that can inspire others to live positively.
137. Skill takes time and practice, and I am willing to work for it.
138. I think like the person I intend to become.
139. I am strong and will live past the difficult times.
140. Of all the paths available to me, I always choose the positive one.
141. Changing myself for the sake of a relationship is silly; I am who I am, and other people love me for it.
142. I am happy with where I am today and am excited about what the future has to offer.

143. I am committed to learning from the best teachers, trainers, mentors, and coaches.
144. My youthful spirit is reflected in the mirror every day.
145. I transform my anxieties into energy, which helps me to conquer my fears.
146. Through the power of my thoughts and beliefs, I am keeping my mind agile and my body healthy and strong.
147. I start every day by shifting my mind into a positive state about my job; I love my work and enjoy the tasks I complete each day.
148. I use my strength and uniqueness to excel and grow. I am proud to show everyone who I am and what I am worth.
149. I am a problem solver and have confidence in the solutions I create.
150. I am naturally curious and pay close attention to others.
151. I find creative ways to get the support I need.
152. Every day, I am looking at the world through a lens of maturity, which opens more doors to greater personal and professional success.
153. I have achieved my goal and am ready to take on the next challenge.
154. Every day, I find more and more reasons to love my job because I am agile, resourceful, and destined for success.
155. I have a huge passion, strength, ability to learn and grow, and it drives me to success.
156. My job is sometimes challenging, and I always find new ways to turn challenges into victories.
157. My job is a vital part of my life and personal growth.
158. I work well under pressure, and my abilities allow me to succeed.
159. I believe in my ability to work with myself and others, and I know that we support each other.
160. I enjoy the progression of my age, and every day, I am turning into a better version of myself.

161. I am grateful for my life's trials, which have helped me to mold myself into the person I am today.
162. I am grateful for the chance to become a better version of myself by living healthy, with a strict diet, and regular exercise.
163. I am grateful for the shelter that I have and the warmth of my life, family, and friends.
164. I accept myself and know that I am capable of great things and worthy of them.
165. I release my fears and worries; I am living my full potential.
166. I am willing to step outside of my comfort zone and try new things.
167. I choose happiness, even when it may be difficult to do so.
168. I am self-assured and courageous; I live in the moment and look forward to what the future will bring.
169. I love who I am and am excited about whom I will become.
170. I trust myself and my choices.
171. My dreams will be achieved through my knowledge and resources.
172. I accept everyone as they are and know that everyone is doing their best.
173. When I do something that makes me happy, I make sure to give myself credit for understanding the pleasures in life.
174. I attract the perfect career for my talents.
175. Every action I take moves me towards my perfect career.
176. I am happy to be paid well for the work that I do, and I know that my job keeps me excited and feeling important.
177. I am open and interested in any new potential career opportunities to further my professional skill set.
178. I know that I bring value to the company I work for and am recognized and appreciated for it.

179. I can make positive career moves for myself, and each is more positive than the last.
180. I am thankful for my new career and the positive impact it has had on my life.
181. Changing careers is joyous, easy, and exciting.
182. I know I can inspire others to do a good job with the work that I complete.
183. I am quickly and effortlessly working my way up the corporate ladder.
184. I am aware of what I have to offer the world and want to share my abilities with others.
185. I accept my body just the way that it is and would not change a thing.
186. I love the features of my body that make me unique, and I see the beauty in them every day.
187. I am beautiful just the way I am and perfect in my own right.
188. I treat my body with love and kindness.
189. I understand when my body needs to rest, and I am always patient with it.
190. I am filled with self-confidence, am positive, and have a prosperous mind.
191. Abundance comes into my life in surprising and pleasurable ways.
192. Money is a tool that allows me to do good things and help the people around me.
193. I deserve to live a wealthy and tranquil life.
194. Difficult times result in me becoming stronger.
195. When fear tells me to run away, I have the strength to not listen to fear.
196. Only I can determine my true value and worth, and only I can manifest it.
197. I surround myself with people who will understand my choices and hold me up, even when it is hard to do so.

198. I fight for what I love and believe in, no matter the consequences.
199. I am the kind of person who finds it easy to make money.
200. Money is a measure of success, and I am a success.
201. All the money I spend is to bring myself and others joy.
202. I have a loving and wonderful relationship with myself; I know that the key to happy relationships is to have a strong relationship with myself first.
203. I show gratitude for the love in my life and am thankful for those I have around me.
204. A loving and healthy relationship will present itself to me when I am ready.
205. I deserve a generous, kind, and good partner.
206. I am attracted to relationships that are open, honest, and healthy for me.
207. I build and maintain strong and healthy relationships.
208. I am capable of giving and receiving love freely.
209. I visualize a new relationship with my perfect partner.
210. I invite loving, interdependent, and genuine friends and connections into my life.
211. My mind is perfectly tuned to attract a romantic relationship.
212. I am grateful for the love that I can give.
213. My feelings are mine, and valid.
214. I am enjoying learning all there is to know about me.
215. I am grateful for all that I have, and for all that is to come.
216. There is no other magic like my magic; I am powerful.
217. I am good at what I do, and my contributions are valuable.
218. I belong in any room I walk into.
219. I love myself, and I know my worth to the world.
220. I am comfortable with eating what I want and have the power of self-control.
221. I can create a good life with the finances that my job provides, and I am grateful for it.

222. The work that I do brings me great joy, and I am passionate to create value for my company.
223. My voice is needed at the table; I will either pull up a seat or take my own.
224. I wake up every morning feeling refreshed and renewed.
225. As I prepare to fall asleep, I release all my stresses of the day.
226. My sleep is restful and calm.
227. I am giving my body the rest it needs and the rest I deserve.
228. My mind accepts positive dreams.
229. I create an avalanche of financial abundance.
230. Incredible things happen to me every day.
231. I have always been successful.
232. Everything I wish manifests in life.
233. I have everything that I could ever want.
234. I am free to choose what I want to experience in my life.
235. I have more than enough wealth in my life.
236. There is endless abundance in the world, and I have my fair share.
237. I choose wealth and abundance.
238. I always express my thoughts and opinions with confidence.
239. I am an inspiration to others due to my confidence.
240. I confidently speak my mind without hesitation.
241. I live life to the fullest due to my confidence that empowers me.
242. When I see something that I want, I go for it without hesitation.
243. My confidence and self-assurance are a part of my everyday feelings towards myself.
244. People look up to me because I always stay true to myself.
245. I am happy with the person I am becoming and excited for the future.
246. I have a happy life, and my positivity is far-reaching.

247. I love to laugh and see the positive in everything.
248. Happiness is a choice that I make every day.
249. I am very capable of managing any challenges that come my way.
250. There is no such thing as disappointment in my life as I only set realistic expectations.
251. My body and mind will be ready to take on new challenges once I have given them the rest they need and deserve.
252. My thoughts and opinions are valuable to myself and others.
253. My confidence, self-esteem, and self-belief are becoming stronger every day.
254. The world is ready to see the special things I have to offer.
255. Being confident in myself comes naturally to me.
256. Speaking my mind with confidence is something I do naturally.
257. My mind is completely focused on success.
258. I always love, respect, and believe in myself unconditionally.
259. I am always starting conversations and meeting new people.
260. Others cannot help but be drawn to my positive energy.
261. I am capable of accomplishing anything.
262. I accept rejection with a positive attitude.
263. I am dedicated to improving my health.
264. I relinquish all pessimism around accumulating money. I allow my desires to persist in the world through my work.
265. I recognize and embrace building opportunities.
266. I have perfect health.
267. Overcoming illness is easy for me.
268. Others see me as someone who lives a healthy lifestyle.
269. Within and without, I feel balanced and healthy.

270. I am a problem solver and am quick to find solutions to the obstacles that I face.
271. I follow through with what I say I will do.
272. I fill my mind with positive thoughts and knowledge.
273. My emotions are unable to control me, and I do not attach to them.
274. I accept how I am feeling, but my emotions have no control over my actions.
275. My environment is calm and peaceful, and my place of work is surrounded by peace.
276. I am watching myself become the person I was meant to be.
277. I am becoming an inspiration to myself and others as I grow.
278. I quickly engage others in teamwork to optimize results.
279. I will seek out new leadership opportunities.
280. Each day, it becomes easier to speak up and take the lead.
281. I take charge easily, no matter the situation.
282. I am highly motivated, ambitious, and driven.
283. I am naturally motivated and energized at the beginning of every day.
284. Every day, I become more driven, motivated, and ambitious.
285. My mornings begin with positive thoughts.
286. My mind is constantly filled with positive thoughts, and it is easy for me to have positive thoughts all the time.
287. I think positively whenever a difficult situation comes my way because I know that I am stronger than the situation.
288. People around me are "lifted" by my ability to think positively.
289. When life throws difficult situations at me, I am confident in my abilities to remain positive and optimistic.
290. I have plenty of time to complete my work because I will always get a head start on important projects.

291. The projects that I am a part of are completed well ahead of schedule.
292. I like to seize the moment, take action for my future, and attain my desires.
293. I am becoming more productive with each passing moment.
294. I always follow through with my word, and so others are comfortable with relying on me.
295. I pursue what I want in life with confidence and decisiveness.
296. I am full of determination, and because of that, I always achieve my dreams.
297. I always go after the highest possible level of success.
298. I am reaching higher and further every day.
299. I persist even when success seems impossible.
300. I always speak up and tell others what I want.
301. Letting go of the past gets easier every day.
302. I am loving and respectful to others around me.
303. I tend to my personal and emotional wellbeing before I offer my love to those around me.
304. I am open about myself when I want to be and use discretion when I see fit; I know my mind will determine when the times are right.
305. I am ready and willing to face the truth in my relationships.
306. I always persist and go after my dreams with everything I have got.
307. I always see the bright side of life, especially in difficult situations.
308. I nurture a deep sense of internal happiness within myself.
309. I am the one that others look to for reassurance during difficult times.
310. I feel a natural sense of peace and happiness within myself.
311. My mind is disciplined, strong, and capable of anything.

312. The goals that I set have me working until I have completed them.
313. I have ultimate self-control that is growing stronger than ever.
314. My unbreakable willpower is the key to my future incredible successes, and I will be a success story.
315. I can always complete my tasks, and others see me as a hard worker.
316. Difficult projects are not challenging for me as I know how to keep my focus and work through them.
317. One of my greatest strengths is my ability to control myself.
318. I maintain a high level of dedication and focus consistently.
319. Each day, I become more confident in who I am.
320. I will love myself unconditionally, no matter what.
321. I am discovering more wonderful things about myself with each passing day.
322. I deserve to go after my goals and do what makes me happy.
323. Accepting myself unconditionally gives me the power to succeed.
324. I have a natural awareness of all the positive things in my life.
325. I seek out new adventure.
326. What I put out into the universe is what is returned to me. So, I will put out peace, love, and happiness to all.
327. My priorities are clear, and my tasks are completed depending on their importance.
328. My work brings me joy, and I have fun with everything I do.
329. I love my sense of humor and am happy to make others laugh with me.
330. I am happy to be myself in my relationships and with my partner.

331. I communicate my needs clearly and effectively with the people in my life.
332. I am successful every day.
333. I live in the moment and know that the future will be wonderful.
334. My mind can adapt to any situation, no matter the difficulty.
335. I am human and have imperfections; I accept and embrace my imperfections wholeheartedly.
336. I can stay motivated through projects, no matter how difficult they may be.
337. My positive energy and motivation can "boost" all of those around me, and others can feed off of my abundant positive energy.
338. I can instantly get into the right mindset before completing a project because it is easy for me to motivate myself.
339. Being motivated and ambitious is a part of the life I enjoy.
340. My goals will be attained through my power of positive thinking.
341. Others admire that I make things happen now rather than later.
342. I always succeed because I meet resistance with persistence.
343. I am persistent, even in the face of rejection.
344. I continue to persist, even when I experience setbacks.
345. My ability to persist is the difference between success and failure.
346. I have limitless confidence in my abilities.
347. I am a productive, motivated, and highly-driven person.
348. I know what I want to do in life.
349. I am conscientious of what I want.
350. I take the necessary risks to put myself in a successful position.
351. I use my available resources to my advantage.

352. I have a carefully planned, well-thought-out future.
353. I am aware of many components when making decisions.
354. I am mindful of how my decisions will affect my surroundings.
355. I trust myself in making decisions.
356. I am a leader when it comes to making decisions.
357. I love to work hard; hard work is the only way to the top.
358. I am someone who takes responsibility for their actions.
359. I am in complete control of myself.
360. Change is a welcomed aspect of my life.
361. I do things that help me be happier, smarter, and healthier.
362. I attract positive people.
363. I am energetic, alive, and at my ideal weight.
364. I am a worthy human being.
365. I feel good about what I want and need, and I can share this with others in my life
366. I know that I am good enough, and that makes me feel comfortable, confident, and strong.
367. My memory is sharp; I absorb knowledge like a sponge.
368. My belief in myself is unshakable.
369. I am confident and open in all social situations.
370. I believe things always work out for the best.
371. There is a champion inside of me that is ready to come out.
372. I help people to achieve their goals.
373. I choose life, love, and happiness.
374. I spread joy and inspiration wherever I go.
375. Today is going to be an amazing day.
376. I know I have the strength and the power to succeed.
377. I love what I do and would do this even if I did not need the money.
378. I am going to have an extraordinary day today.
379. I appreciate the ones who have helped me as well as those who have crushed me, for I am stronger and better because of them.

380. I am courageous enough to live freely.
381. I create opportunities for myself to succeed.
382. I am important. I am worthy. I am irreplaceable.
383. I have the freedom to make the most of life and enjoy all its beauty.
384. I attract great things into my life just by thinking about them.
385. I have the willpower and mind power to overcome my challenges.
386. I look for great abundance in my life.
387. I work hard and always give one hundred percent effort in all my endeavors.
388. My work is fulfilling and enriching to my life; I work to help myself and others.
389. I do not compromise my values for anyone; I stand up for what I believe in.
390. I am humble but still proud of my accomplishments.
391. I accept all forms of criticism and see this as a chance to improve myself.
392. I have the courage to do the right thing, no matter how big or small.
393. I always see the glass half full.
394. I plan well for the future and accept good fortune.
395. The world is a greater place because of me.
396. My creativity never stops flowing, and I am always one to think of new ideas.
397. I take the time to enjoy each facet of my life and relax when I need to.
398. I always seek new opportunities and am open to change.
399. My mind is plastic; I can learn anything I want to.
400. The world is my canvas on which I am painting my masterpiece.
401. I am comfortable with scheduling my time, and creating time for myself is easy.
402. My mind will find a way to get what I want.

403. I am confident, enthusiastic, and passionate about everything I do.
404. Out of my adversity comes abundance.
405. I am the master of creatively expanding my mind.
406. I attract people because I am interesting.
407. I understand that others may have less than me and will always help those around me in any way that I can.
408. I speak positively about others and am grateful that they speak positively about me.
409. I eat healthy and nutritious food every day because I want to fuel my body with only the best ingredients.
410. I know what I want in life and will work hard to achieve it.
411. I trust in my abilities and believe in myself.
412. I have patience and understand that the best things often take time to present themselves.
413. My mistakes are mine, and I own them; I wear them as a badge and carry them as certificates of knowledge.
414. I crave healthy and nutritious food.
415. Every morning, I wake up feeling happy and enthusiastic about life and the day to come.
416. Anything my mind wishes to do will come true.
417. I only need to focus on the things that are in my control.
418. I place my attention on the next thing to do, and only the next thing.
419. I release the things that are not my responsibility to control.
420. I allow myself to take a break and do something I enjoy.
421. I choose to approach my problems with a calm heart and mind.
422. I cannot change the past or completely control the future.
423. I relax into the present moment, knowing that this is the only thing that needs my attention right now.
424. I know that my voice will add value to any conversation; I will always speak up when I want to.

425. Success is always available to me because I recognize my opportunities and grab them when I can.
426. I always go the extra mile for any task that I complete.
427. Sometimes, I will be wrong, and that is okay; I see it as an opportunity to learn.
428. The success of others is something for me to be inspired by and drives me to reach my goals.
429. I relinquish all pessimism around accumulating money. I allow my desires to prolong in the world through my work.
430. I recognize and embrace building opportunities.
431. I learn from my mistakes, and they make me stronger.
432. Only positive actions and thoughts can change my circumstances, but my anxieties cannot.
433. I know how to let go of past hurts.
434. I always keep tabs on my mood.
435. I let myself undergo improvements.
436. I can achieve what I want.
437. I can support myself if needed.
438. Past hurts will only make me weak; instead, I choose to forgive.
439. The only things that define me are my actions and my intentions; only I can evaluate myself.
440. Every day, I take one step towards my goal and bring myself closer to ultimate success.
441. I use my time efficiently and can manage my time to complete all my tasks.
442. I have learned to trust my intuition.
443. I believe in myself to make positive decisions that will help me achieve my goals.
444. I love my face and all of my features, and I am happy and grateful for my beauty.
445. I am amazed and impressed by my body and my abilities.
446. The only person I compete against is myself; I have nothing to prove to other people.

447. I take steps towards my goals every day; I do not wait until the time is right—the time is always right.
448. The unknown will be my success story, and the untested is my battle that I will win.
449. It makes me happy to receive and give compliments.
450. I am a competent member of my team, and I add value to my work and my colleagues' work.
451. My goals are serious, and I take them seriously.
452. I am not afraid to say "no" to people and will only commit to things that I want to do.
453. I know what is right and stand for it.
454. Constructive criticisms will allow me to improve myself.
455. If I have a way to speak up what I want to, I will do it.
456. I can face challenges head-on.
457. I do not let uncertainty taint my objectives.
458. All I have to do is be realistic with my goals so that I will not be disappointed.
459. I grab every opportunity that is thrown at me.
460. Every mistake is an opportunity to learn.
461. I look up to the success of others as my inspiration.
462. I always choose to make positive decisions.
463. I have flaws in my body, and I choose to accept and love them all.
464. I do not like to compare myself to others; I only have myself to compete with.
465. The time is always right to achieve my goals step by step.
466. I set my priorities straight and follow them accordingly.
467. My mind is strong and versatile; any difficulties I face, I can adapt to them.
468. I believe that all people have flaws, including me—all I have to do is accept all of my flaws.
469. I understand that others may have less than me and will always help those around me in any way that I can.
470. I never speak negatively about others as it will bounce back on me.

471. I eat healthily and choose only the foods that bring good health and long life to my body.
472. I am unique and feel good about being myself.
473. I have a reliable memory and trust myself to recall facts accurately.
474. I am dedicated to finishing my work without being thrown off by distractions.
475. I do not take my mind and body for granted; they are my greatest tools.
476. I do not partake in activities that will only bring me down.
477. I always remember that tomorrow is another day and it will be much better than today and yesterday.
478. I love to challenge myself to try new things that are good for my self-development.
479. I always encourage others to become a better version of themselves the same as they encourage me.
480. I choose to make decisions that will provide me with the best results.
481. I choose happiness and let positive thoughts flow through my mind.
482. I refrain from eating foods that are not good for the body.
483. I always look forward to a new day as I wake up in the morning and start my day.
484. I always want to hear my family and friends' laughter, especially if I am the one to bring it.
485. I stay true to myself when I am in a relationship; I do not pretend to be someone I am not.
486. I always have clear communication with those I interact with, especially family and friends.
487. I am successful every day.
488. I always treasure every second that passes in my life for me to have a better future.
489. I know how to analyze problems and solve them accordingly.
490. I always put actions into my words.

491. I always think positively over worries and concerns.
492. I do not let my emotions take over my world.
493. I always make sure my emotions do not affect my life and judgments.
494. I work in a peaceful and calm environment.
495. Nobody is the same as me; I am the only one.
496. I can rely on my memory; I know that I remember things properly.
497. I do not let distractions affect how I work; I always stay focused on getting the task finished on time.
498. I do not make decisions haphazardly; I know that they will greatly affect my future.
499. I want to live happily, so I live positively.
500. I know my goals; I aim to achieve them all.
501. I know that things will always come at the right time.
502. I share my feelings and desires with others.
503. I feel confident about myself. I can show what I have got because I know myself and trust in that.
504. I have an amazing memory; I can trust it when I have to memorize things.
505. I believe in myself, and nothing can change that.
506. I can interact socially with others because I am confident in myself.
507. I am appreciated for being myself and know that I have something unique to offer the world.
508. I am content that I stay true to myself whenever and whatever the situation is.
509. I aim to live my life as happily and positively as I can.
510. My laughter, happiness, and positivity are contagious, and that is a good thing.
511. I make sure to make every day a happy day.
512. My happiness is my top priority; I ensure to aim for that always.
513. I radiate happiness wherever I am.

514. I do not let sickness linger for too long; I always make sure to get well sooner rather than later.
515. I maintain a good weight that is perfect for my body and will not lead me to danger.
516. I am ready to live my life to the fullest and on my terms.
517. My goals are achievable, and I believe in my ability to attain them.
518. My belief in myself is what drives me forward.
519. I wake up every morning knowing that my day will be filled with excitement and opportunity.
520. I wish only for good things to happen to myself and everyone around me
521. The past is over, and it cannot be changed. I forgive everyone, and I free myself from my past pain.
522. I trust my intuition and know what is best for me.
523. My only enemy is myself, and I refuse to stop myself from achieving my goals.
524. I fully approve of who I am, even as I get better.
525. I only live once so I ensure to live my life to the fullest.
526. I believe in myself; I can attain my goals.
527. I do not have time for being lazy; I would rather be productive.
528. I know that I will wake up each day feeling blessed, and even having another chance to wake up every day is already a blessing.
529. Good things will always come my way and I believe in only that.
530. Every person that I meet and interact with is destined to be a part of my life and there is something beneficial that I can gain from them.
531. Every little thing that happens is inevitable; there are no such things as coincidences.
532. I only take part in activities that bring me joy and improve my outlook or abilities.

533. Today will be better than yesterday and tomorrow will be better than today.
534. I am excited to try new things and seek self-development.
535. I push others to become their best selves and support them on their journeys just like how they support me on mine.
536. I make sure that there is at least one task that I have accomplished every day.
537. I know how to manage my money wisely and keep savings aside for the future and in cases of emergency.
538. I opt to relax in the evening and stay away from distracting things, such as phones and gadgets.
539. I always start my day right and wake up on the right side of the bed.
540. I let myself cry sometimes, especially when most needed; I do not have to bottle up my emotions and keep a brave face.
541. I will cry when I have to cry, and start afresh afterward.
542. I never fail to keep myself healthy and fit through exercise and a healthy diet.
543. I encourage others to stay fit and healthy.
544. I use meditation and mindfulness to have a relaxed and peaceful mind.
545. If my body and mind is peaceful and calm, it will radiate out of my body and surroundings.
546. I am focusing my mind and all of my power on the present moment.
547. I remain calm, especially in times of stress, because I know that nothing good will happen out of panic and anxiety.
548. Whenever I feel angry, I try my hardest to calm myself down.
549. I do not lose control because I remain calm under pressure; I only have to acknowledge that I am angry and let it all mellow down.
550. Whenever I feel angry, I make myself more productive so that all my anger becomes good results.
551. I forgive and forget because I want to live a happier life.

552. I have no problem confronting others and telling them what I really feel.
553. I enjoy a good joke and am always a good sport.
554. If I know that I am right, there is nothing and no one that can stop me.
555. I feel fear because fear is still a great character of a true leader; without it, overconfidence in yourself will keep you blind.
556. I solve my issues logically and realistically.
557. Good things will come out of peace and calmness.
558. I do not let stress and anxiety overwhelm me.
559. I am calm and relaxed when something does not go my way.
560. I love to live in the moment because if I worry too much about the future, I will no longer live a happy life.
561. I keep all the life lessons I accumulated and use them wisely.
562. If I live my life the right way, I will not worry about regrets and pain.
563. I am sensitive to the feelings of those around me.
564. I can understand and empathize with other people's feeling.
565. I believe that I can control what I feel under all circumstances.
566. I love adventure and like to face it head-on.
567. I always look forward in every journey because then I see things in a new way.
568. I know that I am blessed and have something to share with others, especially those who are less fortunate.
569. I am happy being alone and it doesn't make me lonely; it is not the same in definition.
570. I enjoy some alone time because then I can collect and reflect on my thoughts.
571. I can enjoy things even if I am alone; I am confident that I can make and do things without the help of others.

572. I don't let negativity affect me because, if I do, I will only be on the loser's end.
573. I can be successful in my own right, especially if I work hard.
574. I know that I will be successful financially because I believe in myself.
575. I always spend my money wisely because it is hard-earned.
576. I am confident that I can handle my finances and save for the future.
577. I contribute sincerely to make the world a better place.
578. I can always think of new ideas because of my creativity.
579. I can get what I want when I put my will into it.
580. All the things I do, I do passionately.
581. With every storm comes a rainbow.
582. I know how to think outside the box.
583. People are always interested in me.
584. If I have a positive mind, all blessings will come.
585. I concentrate on things that are within my control.
586. I plan whatever is the next priority to do.
587. I know what things I can control and what I cannot.
588. I still enjoy vacation time.
589. I face my problems calmly and with an open mind.
590. Every day that passes means that I have gained a day of wisdom and experience.
591. I give myself permission to have high expectations of myself because I know I will meet them.
592. There are no "do nothing days"; I will accomplish at least one task every day.
593. I make small adjustments in my everyday life that will lead to vast improvements in my future.
594. I always choose quiet and calming activities in the evening.
595. I find it easy to get up out of bed and start my day.

596. I am someone who is easily motivated by my drive and my goals.
597. I know that pain is temporary and that it will pass.
598. I love to exercise every single day and look forward to staying energetic all the time.
599. I am the best example of what it means to be fit and healthy.
600. I can use the power of my thoughts to heal my body and my mind.
601. My body and mind are relaxed and calm.
602. I know that the future is important but today is more important to have a better future.
603. I remain calm under all circumstances even will I am under a great deal of stress
604. I am able to calm myself down and detach from anger.
605. I allow myself to acknowledge my angry feelings without losing control.
606. I can use my anger to my advantage and channel it to become productive.
607. I can regulate my emotions and control them to help me succeed.
608. I am comfortable confronting others and telling them how I feel.
609. I am becoming more courageous with each passing day.
610. I will always stand up for what I believe in no matter who is against me.
611. I have courage in the face of adversity.
612. I use logic to resolve my problems and reduce my stress and worries.
613. Staying calm and relaxed has improved my quality of life.
614. I free myself from all anxiety and stress.
615. I always make Plan B so that I am prepared when Plan A doesn't work out.
616. My mind is focused on enjoying the present moment.
617. I live without regrets and chase everything I want.

618. It is easy for me to let go of my past and have no regrets.
619. I am alert to the feelings of those around me.
620. I am able to understand the feelings of those around me.
621. I have full confidence in my emotional judgment.
622. I enjoy seeking new thrills.
623. I focus on the journey rather than the destination.
624. I constantly remind myself of the good things in my life.
625. I understand that being alone isn't the same thing as being lonely.
626. I am not afraid of being alone and I welcome time with myself and my thoughts.
627. I enjoy my own company and look forward to time for introspection.
628. I work hard and push through negativity and criticism.
629. I have a natural belief in my ability to create wealth and success.
630. I am completely focused on achieving financial success.
631. I am highly disciplined with my money and never spend it impulsively.
632. I am in control of my money and I am excited to be saving for the future.

Here's another book you might be interested in

www.ingramcontent.com/pod-product-compliance
Lightning Source LLC
Chambersburg PA
CBHW030136100526
44591CB00009B/679